THE *Tale* OF AN *Eagle*

TRANSFORMING YOUR LIFE'S HORIZONS

BY KARENEA LAI

POND READS PRESS

Edited by Angela Wiechmann
Mountain image © Canatic
Eagle images © TheMountBirdStudio
Lotus image © Rough Edges Supply Co.

Text is set in Adobe Caslon Pro

ISBN 13: 978-1-64343-512-1
Library of Congress Catalog Number: 2025913463
Printed in the United States
First Edition 2025
29 28 27 26 25 5 4 3 2 1

POND READS PRESS

Pond Reads Press
526 West Seventh Street
Saint Paul, MN 55102
(952) 829-8818

www.BeaversPondPress.com

To Ken

But those who hope in the Lord will renew their strength. They will soar on wings like eagles; they will run and not grow weary, they will walk and not be faint.

—ISAIAH 40:31

Introduction

IN THE BEGINNING, there was an ancient oak tree that swayed with the rhythm of the winds. This massive tree's branches extended high up into the sky. They touched the heavens of the earth—something only a few had ever experienced in their lifetime.

Nestled in deep, to the core of this tree, is a cradle of baby eaglets. Each day and night, they observe the sights and sounds surrounding them. Their landscape is filled with so much life. They have a front-row seat to the world's display of energy.

While in this tree, the baby eaglets learn the art of flight. They open and extend their wings, flapping and hovering with pure delight. They practice in the winds that rustle through the leaves and branches with ease. With each passing gust, the inner muscle fibers that make up the eaglets' wings become stronger.

In time, these eaglets will soar. But for the moment, they are to live in the confines of this nest, this sheltered, cozy space woven together with branches and moss.

High above the eaglets, soaring through the trade winds of time, there is a legendary bald eagle famous for his glides and dives. His face is adorned with feathers of white, and his body is covered in the most magnificent golden hues of spiritual light. His wingspan is mighty in its reach as he soars forth with aerodynamic speed. Each flight he takes through these vast open skies is another opportunity to feel the freedom and courage he holds deep inside.

As time blows on, this eagle feels something calling him from below. It radiates with an energy that heals the wounded areas of his soul. This voice, this presence, talks about love and honored bliss. It draws him to the tree in which his own life began, when he himself was but an eaglet.

Flying to a branch he knows quite well, the bald eagle scans the grassy area, searching for the presence that called him. In the shadows of the day, an image appears. It looks much different than himself.

This is a human girl who lives among these leafy trees. Her emerald-green eyes gaze up in wondrous disbelief at the branch in which he is perched. The bald eagle can feel a love-strong energy flowing from her eyes.

The girl tells him all about her journey and how she once made a wish upon these very skies. In this moment, the bald eagle knows that their coming together is not coincidence but fate. Divine guidance has instructed them to meet up in this time and space.

The girl and the bald eagle sit and converse for what feels like an eternity. As they do, they both understand that this is all part of their orchestrated destiny.

The Tale of an Eagle is what lies in our hearts as we learn to extend and grow and fly through a world of creative, imaginative art. We must embrace the light-essence that shines forth from our souls. It illuminates our way as we transcend into the ages of the old. As we launch from our nests and fly in faith, we will find a golden thread weaving its way through all our setbacks and heartaches. We must learn from these lessons and follow this thread.

So please join me on this journey. It's time to soar.

Meditation

High above the midnight breeze, a song floats among the autumn leaves. Its melody sways along with the beats in my chest as I wait to hear what will manifest. Earth has not always been my home of choice, yet it radiates a light that illuminates my yearning for more. I stretch my wings for one more flight. I take to the air. I become one with the night.

The Nest

OUR NEST IS the framework, the foundation, of how our life unfolds in the grand presence of this tree. Our nest is built upon family dynamics, which are, in turn, built upon traditions and beliefs.

Generationally, we must overcome the stigmas of the past, as these are the stepping stones on the path of correcting the ones who have passed before us. As we evolve with age, we are to step through the hands of time. Everything is temporary. We are just momentary travelers passing through this time and space. We are called to discover the true purpose of why we are here. Each day, we must emerge from the ashes of our past and spark a new future.

We are born into this world as physical beings of creative, conscious light. Once we understand that we have this inner light at our core, we can shine it on the areas in our life in need of spiritual lift. We can take on the new problems that arise in our days. We can see these problems as opportunities to strengthen our spiritual muscles, which yearn to grow in every way.

This intrinsic light dances in our minds and allows us to free ourselves from a world that can feel a bit confusing. Embracing each moment as it flows through time allows us to understand the true nature of our lifetime. And once we learn to embrace and transcend this world and lifetime, we will be ready to move into the next phase of our journey.

I can still remember the moment I left my childhood nest, the moment my own abilities were put to the test. I met my husband at age twenty-two, and I got pregnant right away. This created a new future. Or so I thought.

Unfortunately, God had other plans; this baby ended up being a miscarriage. I had to have a dilation and curettage procedure, also known as D&C. Through this surgical intervention, the little fetus was removed and discarded.

Awakening from this procedure, I was left with an empty womb of pain. I felt violated, dejected, and unworthy as a woman. I couldn't believe that this was my life, as I was just twenty-two.

As the hands of time move us from day to night, we must learn to see that we are major players here in this game they call life. Our objective is to proceed forward in faith, knowing there is a vibrational energy strategically guiding us toward our fate.

Stepping into this ring of life, we must learn to let go of our past, as it no longer serves our present. When we move beyond our stored-up fears and worries, we discover a double portion of joy waiting for us on the other side.

We can start by developing an attitude of gratitude. Gratitude is love flowing freely from our heart. When we live from a place that resounds in love, we become more attuned to the oneness within us all.

Your journey will take on many shapes and forms, yet the *you* inside will stay the same, from the day you are born. Your struggles and setbacks are all part of the plan. They help you evolve as you journey this earthly paradise of a land.

Now let us unravel this tale through time. The eagle is your symbol of hope, looming high above in the expansive blue skies. When you see him gliding and soaring with such ease and humility, remember that you, too, can live a life like this. Allow renewal and passion to circulate through your life, as these two elements will revitalize your spirit, which will, in turn, help you feel more alive.

Take on each day and what it has to teach you. These lessons are unwavering; they will bring you to a place of clarity. Become the person you dreamed of in the days of your youth, and allow the message of faith to reverberate through your soul.

Meditation

Consciousness is the key that surrounds our lives. We are to unlock this door and step through the thresholds of transcending light.

The Edge

THE EDGE IS where we go to challenge our minds in all that we know. It's a place that brings in a new level of clarity. It opens us up to an endless array of possibilities, opportunities, and blessings.

As we move toward this edge each day, however, we must be aware of the fears and worries that can sometimes get in our way. For myself, the edge felt a lot like an anxiety-filled dream.

As I pushed through my days, I learned more about life and how we are all intertwined in the conscious realm of spiritual light. Each of us is connected in a mysterious way. We think of each other throughout the day, which means we must be mindful of our negative thoughts.

I can also vividly remember many moments when others challenged me, their opinions stewing in my head. You see, the outside world constantly tries to tell you who you ought to be.

Your job is to let these opinions sift through you. Regardless of what others may say, never forget that you are a gift to this life. There will only ever be one of you, so let that truth be your guiding light. If you can be kind and loving to yourself, that kindness and love will extend to everyone else.

I have faced my edge. As you move toward your own edge, there will be many bumps in the road. These may seem like obstacles and setbacks, but they're actually checkpoints to ensure you're going the right way. When times get tough, you are called to persevere, to dig down deep and station yourself in the spiritual rough. These bumps in the road are your secrets to life. They show you how to overcome adversity and how to reach further into your true promised land. It's all part of the plan.

Divine experiences will surely flow your way as you learn to open your awareness, seize the moments of each day, and immerse yourself in thoughts of joy and peace. These are the positive ingredients that will help you become exactly who you are to be.

Take a moment each day to quiet the chatter

of your mind so you can reflect upon the gifts and blessings you've been given in this physical form of a lifetime. Do not forget that these gifts have expiration dates. Time is always progressing in a forward motion. No matter how hard you try to cling to the past, the door to this lifetime will eventually get permanently sealed inside of eternity.

As you reflect upon your blessings, be sure to embrace the family and friends who surround you each day. They, too, are a temporary part of your experience. As humans, it can be hard to let go of those who have passed, especially the individuals who have played such a major role on our spiritual paths.

Rather than cling to these passed souls, I believe we must encourage them to say goodbye. They are now moving forward on their next journey, to the other side. Adventure awaits them as they consciously expand their reach. They are now free to embody a whole new identity.

The closer you come to the edge, the more

you need to consciously allow yourself some time each day to think, to reflect, to open to joy and peace. This will allow you to be mindfully present in every moment of your life.

When you can live from this place that is lined in peace, you will feel the world move right under your feet. You will feel an effortless essence that transcends your mind and spreads grace and tranquility to all mankind.

Your physical existence is a gift in itself, especially as you learn more about your life and how it has shaped you into a person of prosperity and spiritual wealth. At your core, you are an extension of the purest light. It radiates through and out of you. It provides a way for more and more life.

Meditation

Move toward the edge, and look inside to all that you know. This is where you will find the light that will bring you to the place of your soul.

The Winds

THE WINDS . . . they blow in from east to west. They clear a way for you to manifest.

These breezes . . . they carry what you need as well as what you sometimes dream. You must learn to listen when they pass. They hold the keys to your future as well as to your spirited past. They echo and shift with the changes of time.

The winds . . . they allow you to see into the human fortress that has been designed for you—your outer disguise. As age comes upon you, this disguise unravels, and you with it. More and more, winds open you up to an energy that has been with you since before you were born.

I can still remember the breeze from when I was young. I remember the warmth of its movement and the sound of its pitch. I held out my arms and embraced the wind with a great big hug. In that moment, I felt more alive than I'd ever felt before.

As a child, I often ran outside and played. I'd make believe that I was an explorer who had discovered many lands far, far away. I'd set forth through the forest with my brother by my side. We explored every part of this forested world with curiosity. We took notice of the branches and leaves and how they seemed to rhythmically guide us along our path of make believe.

It's funny how certain moments seem to stand still when you're just a kid. It's as if nothing really matters except your playtime and games. Your imagination is free to roam from one creative expression to the next.

This playful experience is where you first learn who you are inside. This is how the winds open your human treasure chest. Layer upon layer, you unravel the secrets of your mind, and you see the narrative that has been guiding you your entire lifetime.

This is when you realize that, in any given moment, you have the right to choose what you think. Truly, this is your greatest superpower in the world of manifested things.

As your days turn into weeks and your weeks turn into months, you see how the algorithms of life have brought you through challenges and struggles. In these difficult moments, you find your truth—it's represented by a thin golden thread weaving its way all around you. The light of your being and truth emanates at all times. No matter what kind of darkness falls your way, the light will always outshine.

You must stay the course and hold on throughout the fight. The wind will be at your back, guiding you along. It will ensure that you live on and complete the voyage within you.

Seasonally, life changes at a rapid speed. As if you are caught up in a whirlwind, everything fluctuates and transitions all around you, giving you new perspective on your outer shell-like case.

Life is a teacher. Lesson after lesson, you gain deeper understanding of your inner fundamental truths. Lesson after lesson, you gain clarity as to the purpose inside of you.

Meditation

Passing through each mountain and tree, the wind speaks to the soul of who I am, what I do, and who I can be.

The Sun

HIGH ABOVE OUR cloud-filled sky, up in the atmospheric divide, the sun resides. It's been there since the turn of time, and it'll be there after we've passed through this lifetime.

The sun is a symbol of hope. Its rays burn out the darkness and the fear of the unknown. When we sit and bask in the rays of light, we connect to an inner world of spiritual wisdom and insight. In this place of light and love, we feel at home with who we are and who we are to become.

Not so long ago, I felt hindered by the darkness of my present and my future. The further I strayed from my past and my true self, the more my inner light dimmed.

To outside appearances, I was a wife and a mom. On the inside, though, I was merely pretending to be who society said I was supposed to be. I tried to be in control of this fake life I'd created, yet I felt stuck, ashamed, and suppressed. The pressure and the lies were suffocating.

I was constantly critiqued and criticized.

Nothing I did was ever right, no matter how hard I tried. Every time I talked, I was shushed and mocked into silence. I was afraid to even open my mouth. I pretended everything was fine, yet I was a broken vase, glued back together too many times, leaking through the cracks.

In time, I slipped down a spiral of negative, destructive thoughts. Nearly every night, I broke down, sobbing in my pillow, wishing this were all just a dream. I wanted to be free. My spirit called out as I lay there in the chains of my own fright. I wanted to find my inner light, yet it seemed so far away.

But then I saw a light. Its rays illuminated the darkness. Where was this light coming from?

It was coming from me.

It was *my* light. The light of my dreams and ideas and creativity.

I found my way out of that deep place and back to life. I saved my own soul.

I came to understand that my life is a gift. I learned to go deeper within myself and bring forth my light. It became the cosmic root of my life.

It was a new dawn within my soul and within my world. Every morning, I watched the sun greet the day with its rays. This light, this spectacle, this purest form of love transformed me.

You, too, are meant to bring forth your true light. You are to discover your real nature so it can illuminate your life and the world.

Like me, you may struggle with this. Confusion and weakness may cloud your view. It's all too easy to deny your light and to believe you're a failure with no real reason to live.

When I found myself in that deep, dark place, I had to challenge the old ways that had wreaked havoc in my life. I had to undo all the lies I'd been telling myself. I had to free myself from the heavy weight of shame. I had to become one with the conscious mind deep within my brain. I had to rise from the ashes of pain.

You can do the same.

This is the journey of growth and maturation

we all must experience. We are to walk by faith and by the inner light of our soul. When we connect to this calm and peace, we'll connect to the heart of the universe—and more.

Your light is as powerful as the sun. It carries unlimited energy and awakens you each morning to a new feeling of love and surprise. The more you embrace these rays of light, the more they'll guide you toward your purpose as well as your meaning in life.

Meditation

As we live in this realm of day and night, we must adapt to the rising and the falling of the sun's light.

The Cave

HIGH ABOVE THE hills is a place where we can sit and contemplate our life. We call this place the cave. It holds all the answers to the thought-provoking questions we have about our lives.

When we want to access this cave, we must first close our eyes to the realities of the outside world. Next, we must calm the seas of our minds, as they are always in motion with our feelings. Only then can we enter the cave, a place of complete serenity and joy.

The awakened ones are those who have traveled these conscious caves of the mind. In their moments of reflection, the awakened ones grasped the truth that they were on a great quest to connect to their higher ideals.

The awakened ones are people who have persevered through great adversities. For them, every setback was actually a setup in the making. It meant they had to keep moving forward, keep pursuing their new ideal, and keep trusting that challenges and obstacles were simply part of the process.

Adversity also required the awakened ones to examine their personal relationships. They understood that relationships are mirrors on the outside revealing who we are becoming on the inside.

Through the practice of meditation, I was able to enter my own inner cave of peace, a place where I could be with myself and breathe. There were no expectations or criticizing words in this cave—just a harmony of love that made me feel understood.

As I practiced this meditative art each day, an alignment took place. As I became more aware of the things that brought me joy and bliss, everything about my life shifted and changed. I began to feel the universal One.

Life is a continuation of images and scenes. Each picture creates a certain imprint upon our memory bank. And over time, these pictures expand our view of this world.

Every day, we have the opportunity to enter the cave and open ourselves to this new view and awareness. Every day, we have the opportunity to emerge from the ashes of the past. Every day, we have the opportunity to step into our new future with confidence that we are on the right track.

Just beyond the cave is a magnificent oak tree that sways with the breeze. Its branches extend high into the sky while the roots burrow deep into the earth.

Within the canopy of its limbs sits a golden-eyed eagle. His journey has taken him down many paths, each one necessary for his growth. His journey has taken him to the cave. And now he can feel his heart beating within his chest as he eagerly awaits what is yet to manifest.

Les Brown once said, "If you do what is easy, your life will be hard. But if you do what is hard, your life will be easy." Let's face the truth here: the longer you live, the more you'll change and the more the real you will emerge and appear.

But only if you're willing to enter the cave and allow it to awaken you.

The cave truly saved me. It led me to go into myself to reinvent who I was and who I wanted to be, no matter what adversity I was facing. If you have the courage and the strength to trust the cave and to lean into your suffering, you, too, can live a life of purpose and peace.

Meditation

Embrace the quiet moments of your solitude. These moments allow you to connect with the soul light illuminating the space within you.

The River

CRYSTAL WATERS. ROCKY shores. The river is free to flow at the most delicate speed. It spreads forth and brings nourishment to all who thirst and yearn for a sip of insight. The river transcends our world and fills it with love and the most magnificent light.

The eagle perches in a tree near the riverbank. The eagle watches how the river effortlessly flows and how the fish freely swim in its magnificent glow. The fish and the current become one. It's an underwater dream.

The eagle's life depends upon these waters. The river brings in new nutrients and releases old sediments. It's a natural filtration process, a vital renewal. The river keeps itself clean and clear so life above and below the surface may multiply and grow.

When you gaze deeply into these waters of blue, you'll recognize an energy essence, a spirit. You carry this energy essence as well. A river moves and shifts within you too.

Sometimes your river flows and rages,

especially after a torrential storm. Other times, it is completely serene and at peace, like a gentle stream reflecting the sunshine.

If you follow the river within, it'll take you on a journey to your own inner awakening and transformation. Your river carries you along, guiding you to all your hopes and dreams while also clearing out the negativity you hold deep inside.

This channel is your intuition. It's your source to the spirit-light, which connects you to your true self once again. It allows you to understand your true meaning and purpose within this life.

When I think about how these waters have flowed through me, I see how they preserved and shaped the person I was to become. I was destined for greatness. This was the plan. Yet I had to break through a lot of rocks and sticks before my current could flow at its fullest force. My past helped me face my fears, which was all part of my greater purpose.

Through it all, I felt waves of light pass over

me, creating a spiritual awakening of my inner dreams. You see, life itself can feel like a dream, like a movie playing out before us and within us. We have to find our way through each and every one of these scenes.

Your river will teach you all you need to know. It'll teach you who you are. When you are ready to gaze, like the eagle, deep into that river, it'll lead you to the place within your soul that is filled with beautiful light. The light and the water will help you renew your life and transcend.

Meditation

Within each and all of us is a river that flows along with time. It tells the story of our soul, our light, our life.

The Desert

THERE'S A PLACE we all must go to understand life and its chambers of self-discovery and yearning. You must enter the desert of diamond crystals and golden sands. You must listen to the whispers floating upon the breeze. These whispers tell the story of a life longing to be freed—your life.

There's something special about this ancient desert land. It holds the secret to your future self's ability to become something great. We each possess this ability. You will awaken yours once you understand your true value.

The path through the desert isn't easy to master. It takes many bends and turns. Sometimes it feels like a never-ending dream. It goes on for miles and miles, with no oasis to be seen. You will be tempted by illusions—and disillusions.

To make it through this desert, you must be persistent and dedicated. If you call upon your courage and might, you can forge your way across the sands. Step by step, you must walk with faith, learn your truth, and grasp the meaning of the experiences unfolding all around you.

It's a journey to seek that which is deep within. In time, you'll reach the inner place of the soul, the place that holds the light that illuminates your way in this world. With this light in hand, you can finally see the person you've been all along and can now fully be.

But this is not the end of the journey. The path continues, inviting you to walk with your true self and your true calling. Once again, you will need persistence and patience. There will be trials and tribulations, crossroads and challenges.

My own journey through the desert led me to discover who I really am. I found my way to that quiet place of solitude, the source of my inner childhood light. This light spread forth for miles and miles, much like the desert itself. For the first time in my life, I could relax. I felt understood.

You see, I've always been a bit different. I have a unique view of the world. I've always been able to see through the different patterns that make up most people's lives. I can see the limiting beliefs that keep many people in a strange state of resentment. It seems to smother them like a heavy blanket.

Before I entered the desert, I felt that same resentment weighing down on me, hindering me. So I set my eyes on a new way of living, one free from that state of regret. The choice was simple, yet the journey was grave. My path through the desert tested me almost each and every day.

But that's the purpose of this desert. It's here to teach you how to live truly and fully. Each and every day, you must place your best foot forward with courage and persistence. Each and every day, you must journey deeper and deeper into the desert—and deeper and deeper into yourself.

You'll find refuge in the desert as you make your way toward a more fulfilling life. As with any journey, there will be times when it'll bring you to your knees. But those experiences will mold you into the warrior you were always meant to be. The desert will unlock the inner strength you need to endure most anything life throws at you.

Meditation

Empty spaces fill these sands, while the winds blow and extend their love.

The Mountain

A MOUNTAIN IS stacked time. Each layer is built upon the last—from the roots stretching deep into the earth to the summit soaring high into the heavenly glow.

This is the essence of life as well. It's built layer by layer, with both beauty and sorrow combined.

In the journey of life, each and every person comes upon some sort of mountain. It's yet another opportunity to reveal who we are on the inside and to evolve within this realm of time and space. The higher we climb, the higher we'll transcend into new awareness, new consciousness.

But only a few rare souls will accept this path of mountaineering. That is, only a few of us will choose to endure the pain necessary to learn life's lessons. And the hardest lesson of all is learning to let go when a loved one transitions from their earthly body to the light of the eternal world.

I stand now at the foot of the mountain and gaze up. Gliding high above is an eagle carrying a man who has just transitioned into the realm of eternal life. This man's name is Ken.

He was my stepdad.

Ken had such an influence upon me that I can't remember life without him. Letting go of his bachelor status, he chose to take my mom, my brother, and me under his wing. He became a father to us kids. He showed us kindness and love. He was steady in all that he was.

The days, the weeks, and the years flew by. As my brother and I entered new chapters of our lives, Ken's loyal heart was still with us, each step of the way. Once we became parents ourselves, he taught our kids how to love from the heart. Being a grandpa was such an honor for him. It allowed him to extend his wings even farther to embrace us all with his abundant love and might, no matter how far apart we were.

Ken's journey is now complete. He's been freed from this world of limitations and struggle so he can enter a world of endless light and possibility. The memory of his life is ingrained in our souls. It's a treasure we'll carry in our hearts as we continue with our own journey.

As you journey through your own life, make sure to embrace all the mountains that stand before you. They're the pathway to your inner light.

Also make sure to embrace those you love, as they may not get to see another day. Life, reality, time—it's all fleeting. We can be here one moment and gone the next, in the blink of an eye. We never know when our time is said and done.

The present moment is a precious gift. So, too, is the summit of a mountain we've dared to ascend. Only from the top can we see that life is beautiful.

Meditation

In the misty morning, there arose a light that transcended through the shadows, pointing and providing the way for new life.

The Lake

ETCHED ALONG THE landscape of life is a lake. There's something magical and mysterious about this lake. It's a mirror, a reflective pool of golden liquid light.

Perched beside this lake is an eagle. His bones ache, and his feathers are worn from the years that have passed. Still, his eyes glisten with life and wisdom.

Peering into the water, the eagle sees a reflected image that has been buried deep within his soul. It's a vision of his eternal self, the self he was before he was placed in this earthly world. It's a reminder that this physical life is only his temporary home.

Like the eagle, you must gaze upon the glassy surface of the lake. When you do, you'll see an image that is ancient yet ageless. You, too, will see your eternal self, the real you who has always been and will always be. The reflection will awaken your mind to a new kind of beauty, one that allows you to see your true light, your true colors.

You'll also see a reflection of the different dimensions of who you've been in this lifetime. The mirror reveals all your weathered days and sleepless nights, all your moments of faith and fear. It shows how you've persevered, even in the moments when you couldn't make sense of your own inner light.

The chapters of your life are like waves rolling onto the lakeshore. These waves leave behind sandy sediments and change the shoreline right under your feet. In the same way, the days, weeks, and years come and go. They leave behind memory sediments and transform your inner landscape. With the hands of time moving at a steady speed, you must learn to embrace each day's lesson as it washes upon you.

I came upon this lake when I was going through a rough patch. I peered into its mirrored waters and saw a woman in white. She glowed with a cascading essence that I recognized as my eternal soul's light. This woman had known me for ages, even before the day of my birth. She'd waited for me so we could journey this life together and become one with the consciousness of the earth.

I knew then that I'd never been alone, no matter how hard my life had been.

As you cast your eyes over these waters, you'll find that the lake is filled with divine energy. It emanates with a light that helps you transcend to a state of peace, insight, and consciousness. You're filled with that same divine energy, as we were all created in the image of God's eternal light.

The more you embrace this light, this truth, and this present moment, the more you'll understand that we're all just travelers on this earthly land. The more you gaze into these waters, the more your mind will awaken to this beauty. You'll discover that you're more than just a body; you are a spiritual light being.

Meditation

Wave upon wave and reflection upon reflection, these waters grant us the ability to understand life and who we are on the inside.

The Streams

GENTLE STREAMS OF golden light steadily flow throughout our days and nights. They fill us with grace, peace, and love. These streams are made of the same eternal light found in our soul. This light connects us to a much higher level of consciousness and comprehension than we can reach on our own. Through clarity and clairvoyance, these streams illuminate our innermost dreams and reveal the path to another world of mindful solitude and release.

Perched in silence, a golden eagle watches these streams of light ebb and flow above him. A visceral state of awareness rises within him, drawing his attention to the earth energies rising up through his taloned feet. A great wave of release channels through his heart, freeing him from the unconscious self he once thought he had to be.

This is the power of awareness, of intention, of the streams.

I vividly remember gazing up into the skies when I was twelve. I wondered what was beyond that blue background, what allowed the clouds to float by so effortlessly. Though baffled, I could still sense a magical yet conscious presence in the sky. I somehow knew it connected everything in this world and beyond.

As the years went on, I learned to gaze at people in the same way I gazed at the skies. I became an observer of life, watching the people around me react to each experience that came to light. When I looked into their eyes, I saw a cloud hovering over them—a cloud of unconsciousness. These people had no control over their own lives and no awareness of who they were.

I, too, found myself under this same unconscious cloud as I started the journey of raising my own family. Time seemed to just slip away, out of my reach and out of my control. For many years, the dark cloud kept me from seeing the streams of light.

In time, though, I looked up into the skies and spotted those same streams of light I'd seen

Meditation

Streaming light, guide my soul. Direct me toward the journey that I must embark upon and understand.

Epilogue

TIME IS LIFE'S currency. We spend time as if it were money. But they are not the same. We can make more money; we can't make more time. Time is fleeting. Life is fleeting. We must spend this currency wisely.

And so we have come to the point in our journey when you and I must extend our wings and reach for the edges of the vast blueness. I invite you to take to the skies with me.

Together, let us see and hear with clarity—free from worry and fear.

Together, let us live in peace and harmony with ourselves and with all mankind.

Together, let us tap into our intuition, the sense that makes the veil semitransparent so we may live in both the physical realm of our day-to-day life and the spiritual realm surrounding us.

Together, let us find the strength to rely upon the supreme power that has always resided within us and has always pulled us higher and higher.

Together, let us focus our conscious attention on whatever lesson the present moment has to offer and move toward the next stage of existence.

It is time to soar.

Meditation

Golden hues of spiritual light extend throughout the reaches of life. They surround us from the day we are born and give light to the journey that is to be endured.

Acknowledgments

IN WRITING THIS book, I was deeply moved by the journey of my own soul—a journey that seemed beyond the reach of my awareness yet played a huge part in my creation. There is something very magical about this life and how it always seems to guide us back in.

To my family, I would like to thank you all for giving me the space to create each morning and to truly live out my dream of being an author. I will forever be grateful for each and every one of you.

Mom, thank you for allowing me to cultivate my passion and for giving me the freedom to find my purpose. You are and have always been my greatest cheerleader.

Alex, thank you for standing by my side the last twenty-three years. You have supported and encouraged me every step of the way.

Katelyn, thank you for being such a bright light in my life and for filling me with laughter and love.

Kailey, thank you for being my motivator on the days that are tough. You always have such a way of lifting my spirit.

Austin, thank you for showing me the true meaning of joy.

To my editor, Angie Wiechmann, thank you for taking on my project and helping me bring it to fruition. You believed in me when I doubted myself, and you truly gave me wings to fly.

To my readers, thank you for your ongoing loyalty and support of each of my books. Your stories and comments have helped me continue on with my journey of writing.

About the Author

KARENEA LAI is a unique modern-day writer and poet. She found her voice in her published books, *The Tale of a Feather* and *The Tale of a Butterfly*. In these books, she paved the way to express herself and the channel she held within the divine. Karenea had a humble Midwest upbringing that allowed her to truly find herself and connect with the inner voice that has guided her ever since. With her intrinsic ability to captivate and inspire through words, she helps you connect with your higher self so you can ultimately find your own inner peace. Karenea once again invites you on this journey to enlightenment. Her hope is that you, too, will find your own path and cultivate a fulfilling life.